# Twenty to Stitch

# Jelly Roll Scraps

## Carolyn Forster

Search Press

First published in Great Britain 2014

Search Press Limited
Wellwood, North Farm Road,
Tunbridge Wells, Kent TN2 3DR

Reprinted 2014 (twice), 2015, 2017, 2018, 2020

Text copyright © Carolyn Forster 2014

Photographs by Paul Bricknell at
Search Press Studios

Photographs and design copyright
© Search Press Ltd 2014

ISBN: 978-1-84448-946-6

## Suppliers

If you have difficulty in obtaining any of the materials and
equipment mentioned in this
book, then please visit the Search Press website
for details of suppliers: www.searchpress.com

*Dedication*
*For Tina,*
*and all the fun times we had growing up.*

## Acknowledgements

With thanks to Katie French and Roz Dace
for offering me the chance to stitch and play
in order to make such fun things for the
book. Jelly Rolls aren't just for quilts!

# Contents

# Introduction

Jelly Roll™ is the fun name given to a roll of pre-cut strips of fabric designed by Moda, the American fabric manufacturer. It is a great way to buy coordinated fabrics that are already cut into useful 2½in (6.5cm) wide strips.

Lots of us make quick and exciting patchwork quilts from Jelly Rolls, and sometimes there will be odd pieces left over. Instead of assigning these to the waste bin, save them up and you will soon have enough to stitch some of the varied and quick projects in this book. Of course, there is nothing to stop you cutting your own fabric to the required sizes, and you can even buy Mini Charm™ packs that instantly give you a good selection of ready-cut 2½in (6.5cm) squares.

There is something for every mood and occasion in this book. The projects range from bags to bunting, pincushions to pillows (take a look at the adorable Patchwork Dog on page 8 and the Tabby Cat Cushion on page 44), and they make fantastic gifts as well as pretty and practical little things to keep for yourself.

All the projects are designed to be easy to stitch and fun to work on using basic sewing, patchwork and quilting techniques. So look through the tips and techniques on page 48, decide what to make, and in no time at all you will have transformed those scraps you might otherwise have discarded into something beautiful.

## Note:

All of the projects require a basic sewing kit consisting of:

- sewing needles
- pins
- a ruler or tape measure
- a small pair of scissors
- a pair of fabric scissors
- sewing thread.

# Templates

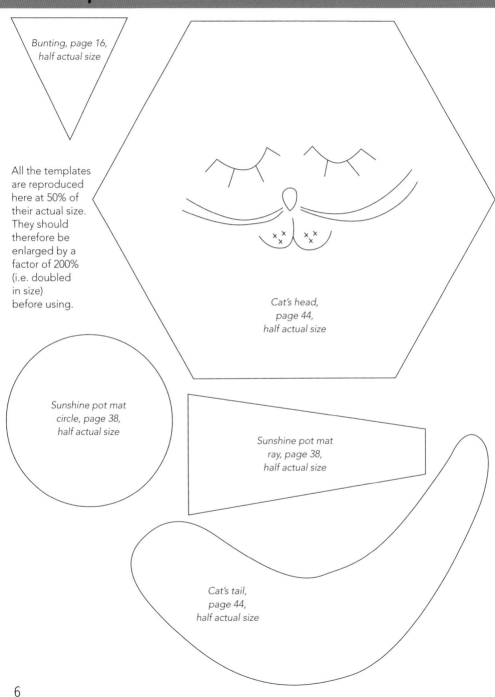

*Bunting, page 16,
half actual size*

All the templates
are reproduced
here at 50% of
their actual size.
They should
therefore be
enlarged by a
factor of 200%
(i.e. doubled
in size)
before using.

*Cat's head,
page 44,
half actual size*

*Sunshine pot mat
circle, page 38,
half actual size*

*Sunshine pot mat
ray, page 38,
half actual size*

*Cat's tail,
page 44,
half actual size*

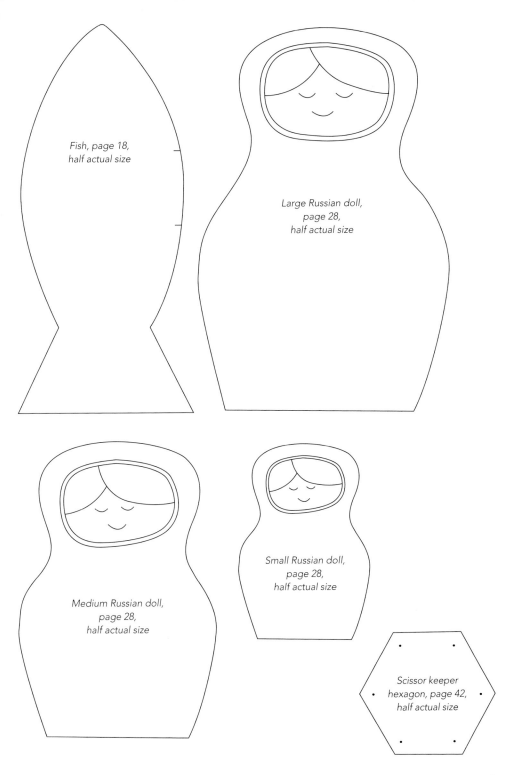

Fish, page 18,
half actual size

Large Russian doll,
page 28,
half actual size

Medium Russian doll,
page 28,
half actual size

Small Russian doll,
page 28,
half actual size

Scissor keeper
hexagon, page 42,
half actual size

# Patchwork Dog

## Materials:

50 squares cut from Jelly Roll scraps, 2½ x 2½in (6.5 x 6.5cm)

Connecting fabric strip, 2½ x 58in (6.5 x 147cm). This can be made of shorter lengths, joined with seams pressed open

4 buttons for eyes, 2 x 1in (2.5cm) and 2 x ¾in (2cm) diameter

Polyester toy stuffing or similar

## Tools:

Basic sewing kit

Scissors

Sewing machine

Rotary cutting mat, ruler and cutter (optional)

Pen to mark fabric

Iron and ironing mat

## Size:

12 x 12 x 2in (30.5 x 30.5 x 5cm)

## Instructions:

**1** Lay out the pieces for the dog as in the diagram below. You will need 25 squares for each side of the dog. Remember that each side of the dog is a mirror image of the other.

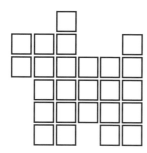

**2** Sew the squares together in vertical rows and press all of the seams open. Place the rows back in their correct positions.

**3** For each side of the dog, sew the rows of fabric pieces together. At the inner corners, leave a ¼in (0.5cm) seam allowance. This will make it easier to turn the corners when you add the connecting strip. Press the seams open.

**4** Now sew the connecting strip to one side of the dog, with right sides facing. First, fold over a ½in (1cm) seam to the wrong side at one end

of the strip and press. Then, starting from the folded edge, sew the strip in place beginning on a long side, such as under the chin.

**5** At the corners, leave the sewing-machine needle in the work, lift the presser foot and turn the work, realigning the raw edges of the fabrics. You will need to snip the joining strip at the outer corners as you reach them.

**6** When you get back to the starting point, overlap the end of the strip with the folded edge by ½in (1cm). Slip stitch the overlap closed by hand.

**7** Now sew on the other side of the dog. This time, where you start and finish, leave a 2in (5cm) gap so that you can stuff the dog. Sew a line of stitches ¼in (0.5cm) from the edge of the fabric on the dog's body only to strengthen this area for stuffing.

**8** Turn the dog right-side out through the opening. Stuff it with toy stuffing until firm, making sure there are no bulges. Slip stitch the opening closed.

**9** Stitch the buttons on as shown in the picture. For each eye, place the smaller button on top of the larger one and sew them in place together. If you are using this as a toy for a child, use felt circles instead of the buttons.

# Bookmark & Book Cover

## Materials:

### For the bookmark

1 Jelly Roll strip, 2½ x 22in (6.5 x 56cm)

1 piece of lightweight iron-on interfacing, 2½ x 11in (6.5 x 28cm)

Stranded cotton embroidery thread to contrast with the fabric

### For the book cover

Jelly Roll scraps, joined to make a strip 2½ x 90in (6.5 x 239cm), with all seams pressed open

Lining fabric, e.g. a linen–cotton blend for extra stability, 9½ x 17in (24 x 43cm)

Notebook, 5½ x 9in (14 x 23cm) with a ½in (1cm) wide spine

Pin brooch/badge to decorate

## Sizes:

**Bookmark**  2 x 10in (5 x 25.5cm),  **book cover**  5½ x 9in (14 x 23cm)

## Instructions:

### Bookmark

**1**  Fold the fabric strip in half across its width, right sides together, and place the interfacing on top, glue-side down. Iron it on to the fabric.

**2**  Trim the end of the strip to a point. Do this by marking the middle and measuring 1in (2.5cm) up each side. Draw a line from the middle to each of these points and cut along the lines.

**3**  Machine stitch the layers together starting at the folded edge. Place two stitches across the point. As you sew back towards the fold, leave a gap of 2in (5cm) for turning through later.

**4**  Trim away the excess fabric at the point and turn the bookmark right-side out. Stitch the opening closed.

**5**  Using two strands of the embroidery thread, hand sew with a running stitch around the bookmark ¼in (0.5cm) in from the edge.

**6**  To make the tassel, wind six strands of the embroidery thread around the fork prongs.When you are happy with the size of the tassel, cut the thread.

**7**  Thread the needle with a length of thread and use this to gather the tassel together between the centre prongs of the fork. Wind the thread tightly and secure with a knot. Take the tassel off the fork and use the thread on the needle to sew it to the point of the bookmark. If you like, you can cut the loops to a tuft.

## Tools:

Basic sewing kit

Scissors

Sewing machine

Rotary cutting mat, ruler and cutter (optional)

Pen to mark fabric

Iron and ironing mat

Embroidery or crewel needle, no. 5

Table fork to make the tassel

## Book cover

**1** From the strip of Jelly Roll scraps, cut nine pieces each 10in (25.5cm) long. Sew these together along the long sides to make one piece. To help keep the overall shape, sew each strip in the opposite direction from the one before.

**2** Press the seams open and trim the piece to 9½ x 17in (24 x 43cm).

**3** Place the piece on top of the lining fabric, right sides together.

**4** Machine around the outside edge, leaving a 2in (5cm) gap in the middle of one of the short sides. Trim away the excess fabric from the corners and turn right-side out. Slip stitch the opening closed and press.

**5** With the lining fabric facing down and the long edges at the top and bottom, fold in the sides of the book cover by 2¼in (6cm). Pin them in place.

**6** Stitch along the top and bottom edges to secure, ⅛in (0.25cm) from the edge of the fabric. Secure the threads.

**7** Turn the flaps right-side out and insert the book to fit comfortably into each flap.

**8** Pin the brooch or badge in place on the front of the book cover to finish.

# Little Drawstring Bag

## Materials:

Jelly Roll scraps, joined to make 4 strips
each 2½ x 21in (6.5 x 53.5cm), with seams
pressed open

Lining fabric, 8½ x 20½in (21.5 x 52cm)

Casing fabric, 2 pieces 2½ x 8½in (6.5 x 21.5cm)

Ready-made cord, 31½in (80cm) long

Cotton perle embroidery thread no. 12 to finish
the top edge of the bag

## Tools:

Basic sewing kit

Scissors

Sewing machine

Rotary cutting mat, ruler and cutter (optional)

Pen to mark fabric

Iron and ironing mat

Embroidery or crewel needle, no. 5

Safety pin for threading the cord through

## Finished size:

8 x 10in (20.5 x 25.5cm)

## Instructions:

**1** Sew the four strips together along the long sides to make a rectangle. Press the seams open. Trim to 20½in (52cm).

**2** Fold the rectangle in half across the width, right sides together, and sew up each side starting at the folded end. Stop 2in (5cm) from the top on each side.

**3** Fold the lining fabric in half across the width, right sides together, and sew up each side starting at the folded end, as in step 2. Stop 2in (5cm) from the top on each side. Leave a gap of 2in (5cm) in the middle of one of these seams for turning through later.

**4** Turn the bag right-side out and place it inside the lining so that the right sides are facing and the side seams are aligned. Match up the top of the lining with the top of the bag and sew each of the two sides to the lining separately.

**5** Snip off the excess fabric at the corners and turn the bag right-side out through the hole in the lining. Stitch the hole closed and press the bag.

**6** Hand sew around the top of the bag with the cotton perle thread using a running stitch to keep it in place.

**7** Make the casing for the cord. Press each fabric strip into thirds. Fold in each end with a double hem to the side of the casing with the raw edge. Machine down.

**8** The casing should measure 7½in (19cm) long after the second end has been neatened. Trim off any excess fabric as required.

**9** Pin the casing in place on each side of the bag, 1½in (4cm) from the top. Machine stitch along each long side ⅛in (0.25cm) from the edge.

**10** Thread the cord through the casings using a safety pin and knot the ends together.

# Thread Pot

## Materials:

Outside of pot: 16 fabric squares cut from Jelly Roll scraps, 2½ x 2½in (6.5 x 6.5cm)

Lining: 4 fabric strips, 2½ x 8½in (6.5 x 21.5cm)

## Tools:

Basic sewing kit

Scissors

Sewing machine

Rotary cutting mat, ruler and cutter (optional)

Pen to mark fabric

Iron and ironing mat

## Finished size:

3in (7.5cm) diameter and 3½in (9cm) high

## Instructions:

**1** Sew four fabric squares together into a row. Make four of these strips and press the seams open.

**2** Lay out these four strips as in the diagram opposite and sew the four central squares together to form the base, stopping ¼in (0.5cm) from the edge of the fabric.

**3** Now sew the edge of each strip to the next one. Stop stitching ¼in (0.5cm) from the end of each seam. When you have stitched together all four strips your pot will be standing up! Press the seams open.

**4** Now sew the lining. Lay out the strips as you did for the outside of the pot and join them together in the same way. Make little snips in the seams at the points where the sides fold up from the base (at the end of step 2). Press the seams open. Leave a gap of about 2in (5cm) in the middle of one of the seams for turning through later.

**5** Put the lining in the pot with right sides facing. Match up the four points and pin.

**6** Sew the lining to the pot at these four points. Sew each one individually.

**7** Snip away the excess fabric at the tops of the points, and turn through.

**8** Sew up the opening and turn down the top of the pot to form a rim. Poke the bottom corners out to form a square base.

# Mini Bunting

## Materials:

Jelly Roll scraps, 2½ x 5in (6.5 x 13cm), about 10 per metre (or yard) of bunting

Tape, ⅝in (1.5cm) wide, as long as your bunting plus 40in (100cm) for the ties at each end

Machine sewing thread to blend with the tape

## Finished size:

Each flag is 2 x 2in (5 x 5cm)

## Tools:

Basic sewing kit

Scissors

Sewing machine

Rotary cutting mat, ruler and cutter (optional)

Pen to mark fabric

Iron and ironing mat

Card or template plastic to make bunting triangle (optional)

## Instructions:

**1** Copy the template on to card or template plastic and cut it out.

**2** Fold each Jelly Roll scrap in half across the width, right sides together. Press.

**3** Take a folded fabric scrap, place the point of the template on the folded edge and mark the two lines that you will sew along to make a flag.

**4** Sew along one of the drawn lines, starting at the edge of the fabric. Make two stitches across the point where you turn to sew up the second side, as this will give you more room to turn the point through. At the end of the second side, instead of finishing the threads move immediately on to the next flag. (This is known as chain piecing.) Sew as many flags as you need to make your bunting. Snip through all the threads.

**5** Trim the seams on each flag to a scant ¼in (0.5cm), narrowing this as you reach the point on each side.

**6** Turn the flags right-side out and press.

**7** Start to pin the flags 20in (50cm) from the end of the tape. This will give you some extra to tie the bunting up with. You will need to leave the same length at the other end. Pin the flags on to the wrong side of the tape just below the centre line of the tape (the tape will be folded over to cover the raw edges of the flags). Space the flags about 2in (5cm) apart.

**8** Now start folding the tape in half to cover the flag tops and so that the edges of the tape meet up. Start sewing about 2in (5cm) before the first flag and 2in (5cm) after the last flag. Secure the stitching.

> ### Note:
> Make a quick variation on this bunting by stitching the flags together right sides together and trimming away the excess fabric on the seams using pinking shears. Attach them to ½in (1cm) wide tape using zigzag stitch.
>
>

# Hanging Fish

## Materials:

### For each fish

4 Jelly Roll strips, 2½ x 8½in (6.5 x 21.5cm)

2 Jelly Roll strips, 2½ x 4½in (6.5 x 11.5cm)

20in (50cm) of ¼in (0.5cm) wide ribbon per fish

2 buttons for eyes, ½in (1cm) diameter

Polyester toy stuffing or similar

## Tools:

Basic sewing kit

Scissors

Sewing machine

Rotary cutting mat, ruler and cutter (optional)

Pen to mark fabric

Iron and ironing mat

Template plastic or thin card to make
fish template

## Finished size:

4 x 8in (10 x 20.5cm)

## Instructions:

**1** Sew two of the long strips together along their lengths. Press the seams open.

**2** Sew one of the short strips across the end of the resulting rectangle, at right angles to the joined strips. Press the seam open.

**3** Make another piece using the remaining three strips.

**4** Copy the template on to card or template plastic and cut it out.

**5** On the wrong side of one of the fabric pieces, place the fish template and draw around it. Decide which way round you want your fish to be – with the shorter strip forming either the tail or the head.

**6** Pin the two sewn fabric pieces right sides together. Take a length of ribbon, fold it in half and knot the raw ends together. Insert the knotted end of the ribbon into the fish, leaving the knot just outside the sewing line.

**7** Starting at the point marked on the template with some reinforcing stitches, sew all the way around the fish along the drawn line, stopping at the second mark with some more reinforcing stitches. Sew one or two stitches across each corner to enable a smoother finish at these points.

**8** Trim the excess fabric away leaving a scant ¼in (0.5cm) seam allowance, snipping the fabric off across the points of the tail.

**9** Turn the fish right-side out and stuff.

**10** When firm, sew the opening closed.

**11** Sew on the two buttons as marked using a strong thread or double sewing thread. If you make these fish for young children, replace the button eyes with felt circles and shorten the loops.

# Flower Hair Snap

## Materials:

Jelly Roll scraps for flower, 2½ x 8in (6.5 x 20.5cm)

Jelly Roll scraps for flower centre, 2½ x 2½in (6.5 x 6.5cm)

Plain hair snap

Self-cover plastic button, 1¼in (3cm) diameter

Felt circle to back the flower, 1¼in (3cm) diameter

## Finished size:

3in (7.5cm) diameter

## Tools:

Basic sewing kit

Scissors

Sewing machine

Rotary cutting mat, ruler and cutter (optional)

Pen to mark fabric

Iron and ironing mat

Craft glue to stick the flower to the clip

Peg to hold flower in place while drying

## Instructions:

**1** Take the strip of fabric for the flower and, with right sides facing, sew the two ends together to form a continuous loop. Press the seam open.

**2** Fold the loop in half along its length, wrong sides together, and press.

**3** With the machine on its longest stitch length, machine around the loop ⅛in (0.25cm) away from the raw edge. Cut the threads leaving long tails. Sew another row close to the first.

**4** Tie the threads together at one end only to secure.

**5** With the other end of the threads, using the top two only, carefully gather up the loop to create the flower. Tie off the thread with a secure knot and trim.

**6** Lay the flower right-side up on the felt circle and stitch through to secure.

**7** Cover the button following the instructions on the packaging. Stitch the button on to the flower centre and secure it to the felt. Make sure it covers the middle of the flower.

**8** Apply glue to the felt on the back of the flower and stick it on to the end of the hair snap. Use a peg to hold the hair snap in place while the glue is drying.

# Stacked Pincushions

## Materials:

For each pincushion, 4 Jelly Roll scraps
2½ x 4½in (6.5 x 11.5cm)

Buttons, 1in (2.5cm) diameter for single
pincushions and 1½in (4cm) diameter
for stacked pincushions

Strong thread or buttonhole twist to
coordinate with buttons and fabrics

Polyester stuffing or similar

## Tools:

Basic sewing kit

Scissors

Sewing machine

Rotary cutting mat, ruler and
cutter (optional)

Pen to mark fabric

Iron and ironing mat

## Finished size:

Each pincushion measures
4 x 4in (10 x 10cm) and is 1in (2.5cm) deep

## Instructions:

**1** Sew the strips together in pairs along the
long sides. Press the seams open.

**2** Place the fabric pieces right sides together
and at right angles to each other. Pin them at
the corners.

**3** Stitch around the outside edges of the
square, sewing one or two stitches across the
corners. Leave a gap of about 1in (2.5cm) in
the centre of one side. At this opening, work
an extra line of machine stitching just within
the seam line on the edge that has the fabric
join. This will stop the seam coming open when
you stuff the cushion and give you a line to sew
along when you close up the gap.

**4** Trim the fabric away across the corners and
turn the square right-side out.

**5** Stuff the cushion until firm, then stitch the
opening closed.

**6** With a long needle and using the strong
thread, sew on the button. Pass the needle
and thread right through the pincushion to the
other side and pull the thread taut to create
a 'dimple' on the top and the bottom of the
cushion. Start with a knot and on the top where
the button will go, and stitch through to the
back and up again before attaching the button.
When the button is secure, loop the thread
around the base of the button, push the needle
as far as you can into the pincushion to lose the
thread and then snip.

**7** Use the same process for the stacked
pincushions. Remember to stack the
pincushions at an angle to each other, and to
use a longer needle if necessary.

# Hair Scrunchy

## Materials:
Strip of fabric 2½ x 25in (6.5 x 63.5cm) made from Jelly Roll scraps, with seams pressed open

9in (23cm) of cotton-covered elastic, ¼in (0.5cm) wide

## Tools:
Basic sewing kit

Scissors

Sewing machine

Rotary cutting mat, ruler and cutter (optional)

Pen to mark fabric

Iron and ironing mat

2 large 2in (5cm) safety pins

## Finished size:
3in (7.5cm) diameter

## Instructions:
**1** Fold the fabric strip in half along its length, right sides together, and sew them together along their length to make a tube.

**2** Secure the safety pin to one end of the tube and push it through the inside of the tube to the other end to turn it right-side out.

**3** Pin the safety pin to the end of the elastic, and with another pin the elastic to the tube end. Insert the elastic through the inside of the tube and when it comes out of the other end, knot the two ends together. This will cause the fabric to scrunch up.

**4** To secure the fabric, fold a ½in (1cm) hem to the inside of the tube at one end. Overlap this with the raw edge at the other end of the tube, moving the knot out of the way.

**5** On the sewing machine, sew through the fold on both sides at once and through the elastic. Secure the threads.

# Plastic Bag Dispenser

## Materials:
20 Jelly Roll scraps, each 2½ x 8in (6.5 x 20.5cm)
10in (25.5cm) of cotton-covered elastic, ¼in (0.5cm) wide
Lining fabric, 20 x 15½in (51 x 39.5cm)
Fabric for hanging loop, 2½ x 8in (6.5 x 20.5cm)

## Tools:
Basic sewing kit
Scissors
Sewing machine
Rotary cutting mat, ruler and cutter (optional)
Pen to mark fabric
Iron and ironing mat
Safety pin for threading the elastic through

## Finished size:
17½in (44.5cm) long and 13in (33cm) diameter

## Instructions:

**1** Sew ten Jelly Roll scraps together along their lengths. Sew the remaining ten together in the same way. Press the seams open.

**2** Lay the two strips together, right sides facing. Make sure the seams are matching and stitch the two strips together, across the seams. Press the seam open.

**3** Place the lining and the bag front wrong sides together. The lining should be shorter than the bag at the top edge. Fold in half lengthways, matching up the raw edges, with the lining inside the tube. Sew a seam ⅛in (0.25cm) from the raw edges. Now turn the tube so that the lining is outermost, roll the seam to even it out and sew along the length of the tube ¼in (0.5cm) from the seam edge. This is known as a French seam.

**4** Along the bottom edge of the tube, turn a 1in (2.5cm) hem to the lining side. Fold in the raw edge and machine round to make a casing. Leave a 1in (2.5cm) gap to thread the elastic through.

**5** Using a safety pin on the end of the elastic, thread the elastic through the casing. Knot the two ends together, adjusting the size of the opening to suit. Sew the hem to complete.

**6** Make the loop for the top of the tube. Fold the fabric strip in half lengthways, wrong sides together, then fold the raw edges into the centre to meet. Press.

**7** Machine along each side ⅛in (0.25cm) in from the edge. Fold in half to make a loop.

**8** Fold a double hem at the top of the tube towards the lining fabric, securing the lining in place. Insert the loop into the hem next to the French seam. Machine around the hem to secure and fix the loop in place.

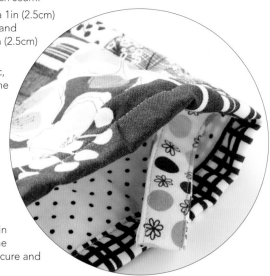

# Russian Dolls

## Materials:

For the small doll, 4 Jelly Roll scraps, 2½ x 4in (6.5 x 10cm)

For the medium doll, 6 Jelly Roll scraps, 2½ x 5in (6.5 x 13cm)

For the large doll, 8 Jelly Roll scraps, 2½ x 6in (6.5 x 15cm)

Polyester toy stuffing or similar

Felt for faces

Stranded black embroidery thread

## Instructions:

### Follow the same method for each size of doll.

**1** Copy the template on to card or template plastic and cut it out.

**2** Stitch half of the scraps together lengthways to make a rectangle for the front of the doll. Stitch the remaining scraps together in the same way for the back. Press the seams on the front piece in the opposite direction to those on the back so they fit together when right sides are facing.

**3** Cut the oval for the face from felt, following the outside line. Draw the markings on to the felt for the features and use two strands of embroidery cotton to stitch them using a backstitch.

**4** Position the face on the front of the doll, with the strips running horizontally. Stitch the face on to the fabric using backstitch.

**5** Lay the front and back fabric pieces together, right sides facing, and use the template to mark the stitching line. Sew along the drawn line, leaving an opening at the bottom for stuffing and turning through.

**6** Trim away the excess fabric leaving a ¼in (0.5cm) seam allowance. Snip the curves to give a smoother line when turned through, and turn right-side out.

**7** Stuff firmly and smoothly, and stitch the opening closed.

## Tools:

Basic sewing kit

Scissors

Sewing machine

Rotary cutting mat, ruler and cutter (optional)

Pen to mark fabric

Iron and ironing mat

Embroidery or crewel needle, no. 5

Template plastic or thin card to make templates

## Finished sizes:

Small, 4 x 3in (10 x 7.5cm)

Medium, 6 x 4in (15 x 10cm)

Large, 8 x 5in (20.5 x 13cm)

# Needle Book

## Materials:

2 Jelly Roll scraps for the cover, 2½ x 7in (6.5 x 18cm)

2 Jelly Roll scraps for the inside, 2½ x 7in (6.5 x 18cm)

Wadding (batting) to line the cover, 2½ x 7in (6.5 x 18cm)

Medium-weight interfacing to stiffen the cover, 2½ x 7in (6.5 x 18cm)

Brushed cotton or felt for the pages, 2 pieces each 4 x 5in (10 x 13cm)

Cotton perle embroidery thread no. 8 for the stitching

Button, 1in (2.5cm) diameter

20in (50cm) of ⅛in (0.25cm) wide ribbon

## Finished size:

3 x 4½in (7.5 x 11.5cm)

## Tools:

Basic sewing kit

Scissors

Sewing machine

Rotary cutting mat, ruler and cutter (optional)

Pen to mark fabric

Iron and ironing mat

Pinking shears

Embroidery or crewel needle, no. 5

## Instructions:

**1** Stitch the two Jelly Roll scraps for the cover together along their long sides. Press the seams open. Do the same for the inside of the book.

**2** Lay the inside piece down, wrong-side up, and place on top the wadding and then the interfacing. Lastly, place the piece for the cover on top, right-side up. Pin the layers to keep them together.

**3** Secure all the layers together by hand stitching around the outside of the case ½in (1cm) from the edge. Use a running stitch and the cotton perle thread.

**4** Trim the edge with pinking shears, just taking off the straight sides.

**5** Trim the two pages in the same way.

**6** Fold the book in half and mark the spine with a pin.

**7** Fold the pages in half and position them down the spine on the inside of the book. Stitch them into position with the cotton perle thread and a backstitch.

**8** Fold the ribbon in half and pin the loop on the inside of the book. Position it in the middle on the right-hand edge, next to the running stitches. Sew the ribbon in place securely.

**9** Sew the button on to the front cover of the book, about ½in (1cm) in from the edge and centred on the seam where the two fabrics are joined.

**10** To secure when the book is closed, wind the ribbon around the button and then around the book. Tie with a bow.

# Buttoned-up Cushion

## Materials:

Cushion fabric, linen or linen–cotton blend, 12½ x 36½in (32 x 93cm)

Jelly Roll scraps to cover buttons, 6 pieces 2½ x 1½in (6.5 x 4cm)

6 plastic self-cover buttons, 1¼in (3cm) diameter

Sewing thread to match cushion fabric

13¾in (35cm) cushion pad

## Finished size:

12 x 12in (30.5 x 30.5cm)

## Tools:

Basic sewing kit

Scissors

Sewing machine

Rotary cutting mat, ruler and cutter (optional)

Pen to mark fabric

Iron and ironing mat

## Instructions:

**1** On the wrong side of the fabric, turn a 4in (10cm) double hem (turn over 2in/5cm and then 2in/5cm again) on one of the short ends. Machine stitch to secure.

**2** On the other short end, turn a 5in (13cm) double hem to the wrong side (turn over 2½in/6.5cm, then 2½in/6.5cm again). Machine stitch to secure, then stitch along the folded edge, ⅛in (0.25cm) in.

**3** On the deepest hem end of the fabric on the right side, mark and stitch six buttonholes. These should be approximately 1½in (4cm) apart. To space them evenly, measure from the middle out towards the raw edges.

**4** Lay the fabric wrong-side up and fold in the edge with the buttonholes by 5in (13cm). Fold in the other end by 10in (25.5cm). The buttonholed end should overlap the longer end. Pin in place and then stitch along the raw edge to secure. You can zigzag to neaten if you like.

**5** Turn the cushion cover right-side out and press.

**6** Make the buttons by covering them in the Jelly Roll scraps following the button manufacturer's instructions.

**7** Mark the button positions through the buttonholes, and stitch the buttons in place.

**8** Insert the cushion pad and do the buttons up.

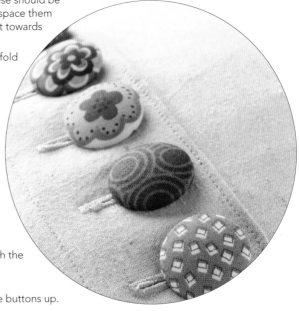

# Itsy Bitsy Bag

## Materials:

9 x 2½in (6.5cm) squares of light-coloured fabric

9 x 2½in (6.5cm) squares of dark-coloured fabric

1 Jelly Roll strip for the gusset, 2½ x 22in (6.5 x 56cm)

Lining fabric, 13 x 7¼in (33 x 18.5cm)

Fabric for loop, 2½ x 3in (6.5 x 7.5cm) cut in half lengthways to make a strip 1¼in (3.25cm) wide

Fabric for handles, 2½ x 22in (6.5 x 56cm)

Button for closure, 1in (2.5cm) diameter

## Tools:

Basic sewing kit

Scissors

Sewing machine

Rotary cutting mat, ruler and cutter (optional)

Pen to mark fabric

Iron and ironing mat

## Finished size:

7 x 7in (18 x 18cm) excluding handles

## Instructions:

**1** On the back of the light squares, draw a diagonal line from corner to corner. Place these on top of the dark squares, right sides facing. Stitch along either side of the line, ¼in (0.5cm) away from the line.

**2** Cut the squares in half along the drawn line and press the seams open. You will have 18 of these in total.

**3** Lay nine of the squares out in three rows of three, with all the seams running in the same direction. Sew the squares together in rows, pressing the seams in alternating directions on each row. Sew the rows together to make a block. Press the seams open. Make two of these blocks, one for each side of the bag.

**4** Stitch the gusset around three sides of one of the blocks, right sides facing. Press the seams towards the gusset. Repeat, sewing the other block to the gusset. Press the seams towards the gusset.

**5** To make the loop for the button fastening, fold the fabric in half lengthways, wrong sides together, and fold the raw edges into the fold. Press and machine stitch along the edge.

**6** Fold the strip in half to form a loop and pin it centrally on the back of the bag on the wrong side, just below the top edge. The loop should be pointing downwards into the bag.

**7** Now make two handles. Fold the piece of fabric for the handles in half lengthways, wrong sides together, and fold the edges into the middle as you did for the loop. Press and machine stitch along each edge to secure.

**8** Cut the fabric in half widthways to make two handles. Pin these on the top edge of the bag, one on each side. Align the raw edges and position them in the middle of the two outside squares. The handles will be facing down into the bag.

**9** To make the lining, fold the lining fabric right sides together so that it measures 6½ x 7¼in (16.5 x 18.5cm) and machine up each side. On one side leave a 2in (5cm) gap in the middle for turning through later.

**10** To shape the lining base, refold the lining so that the seams are in the middle and mark 1in (2.5cm) on either side of one of the seams across the point. Stitch across between these two marks. Secure the stitching and cut off the point leaving ¼in (0.5cm) seam allowance. Repeat for the second seam.

**11** Place the outer bag inside the lining, right sides together. Match the side seams and pin. Sew around the top of the bag.

**12** Turn the bag right-side out, sew the opening in the lining closed and press.

**13** Sew the button on the bag about ½in (1cm) down from the top edge.

# Tissue Pouch

## Materials:

3 Jelly Roll scraps, 2½ x 5½in
(6.5 x 14cm)

Lining fabric, 5½ x 6½in
(14 x 16.5cm)

5½in (14cm) of ½in (1cm) wide
cotton lace

## Tools:

Basic sewing kit

Scissors

Sewing machine

Rotary cutting mat, ruler and
cutter (optional)

Pen to mark fabric

Iron and ironing mat

## Finished size:

5 x 2¾in (13 x 7cm)

## Instructions:

**1** Stitch the three Jelly Roll scraps together along their long
sides to make a rectangle. Press the seams open.

**2** Place the rectangle on top of the lining fabric, right sides
together. Insert the lace along one long edge so that the
majority of it is visible between the right sides of the fabrics. Pin
it in place and sew along the seam to secure the lace within it.
Sew along the second long edge at the other end.

**3** Turn right-side out and press.

**4** Fold into thirds with the lining fabric outermost and the two
finished edges abutting. The lace should overlap the other
finished edge on the inside of the pouch. Pin.

**5** Stitch along the raw edges at each end of the pouch. Zigzag
to neaten if you like.

**6** Turn the pouch right-side out and insert a pocket-size packet
of tissues.

# Sunshine Pot Mat

## Materials:

Assorted yellows from Jelly Roll scraps for the rays, 2½ x 5in (6.5 x 13cm)

Fabric square for the centre, 5 x 5in (13 x 13cm)

Wadding (batting), 13 x 13in (33 x 33cm)

Backing fabric 13 x 13in (33 x 33cm)

Cotton perle embroidery thread no. 12 to quilt the mat

## Tools:

Basic sewing kit

Scissors

Sewing machine

Rotary cutting mat, ruler and cutter (optional)

Pen to mark fabric

Iron and ironing mat

Embroidery or crewel needle, no. 5

Freezer paper for the circle appliqué, 5 x 5in (13 x 13cm)

Template plastic or thin card to make the templates

## Finished size:

11in (28cm) diameter

## Instructions:

**1** Copy the templates on to card or template plastic and cut them out.

**2** Cut 20 rays from the yellow Jelly Roll scraps using the template. Stitch the rays together with right sides facing and with the narrow ends together. Press the seams open.

**3** Lay the wadding down flat and place the backing fabric on top, right-side up. Now centre the circle you have sewn on top, right-side down. Pin to secure around the outside edge.

**4** Stitch all the way around the outside edge of the circle. Trim away the excess wadding and backing fabric leaving a scant ¼in (0.5cm).

**5** Turn the mat right-side out through the hole in the centre. Roll the circle edge until it lies flat and tack all the way around to secure.

**6** To make the centre circle, cut the circle from the freezer paper using the template. Iron this shiny-side down on to the wrong side of the fabric for the centre of the mat. Cut out the fabric adding a ¼in (0.5cm) seam allowance all the way around. Tack the hem on to the freezer paper. Fold the circle into quarters and use these lines to balance and centre the circle over the hole in the middle of the mat by matching the folds with the seams. Pin in place and appliqué down.

**7** As you come to the 1in (2.5cm) of stitching, take out the tacking and remove the freezer paper. Refold the hem and complete the stitching to close.

**8** Using the cotton perle thread, quilt by hand around the edge of the centre circle and then ¼in (0.5cm) away from all of the seams.

**9** Remove the tacking and quilt around the outside of the mat ¼in (0.5cm) away from the edge.

# Patchwork Placemat

## Materials:

42 squares, 2½ x 2½in (6.5 x 6.5cm), or 1 packet of Moda Mini Charms

Wadding (batting), 15 x 13in (38 x 33cm)

Backing fabric, 15 x 13in (38 x 33cm)

Cotton perle embroidery thread no. 8 for quilting

## Tools:

Basic sewing kit

Scissors

Sewing machine

Rotary cutting mat, ruler and cutter (optional)

Pen to mark fabric

Iron and ironing mat

Embroidery or crewel needle, no. 5

## Finished size:

11¼ x 13¼in (28.5 x 33.5cm)

## Instructions:

**1** Lay out the squares in six rows of seven.

**2** Stitch each row of squares together. Press the seams on each row in alternate directions.

**3** Stitch the rows together. The seams should knit together perfectly due to the pressing. Press the seams of the rows in one direction.

**4** Lay the wadding down flat and place the backing fabric on top, right-side up.

**5** Centre the patchwork on top, right-side down.

**6** Stitch all the way round the edge of the patchwork through all three layers. Leave a gap of about 2in (5cm) in the middle of one straight side. Secure the threads.

**7** Trim the backing fabric to a scant ¼in (0.5cm) and trim the wadding close to the stitching line. Trim the corners off at an angle to reduce bulk.

**8** Turn the quilt right-side out and slip stitch the opening closed. Roll the edge of the quilt until it lies flat and tack into place.

**9** Using the cotton perle thread, quilt around the outside of the quilt ¼in (0.5cm) from the edge. Remove the tacking.

**10** To secure the quilt layers, work one cross stitch at each seam junction, letting the needle and thread travel from one stitch to the next through the wadding layer.

# Pincushion Scissor Keeper

## Materials:
Jelly Roll strip for outside edge of pincushion,
2½ x 18in (6.5 x 46cm)

Jelly Roll strip for centre, 2½ x 6in (6.5 x 15cm)

20in (50cm) of ¼in (0.5cm) wide ribbon

Polyester toy stuffing or similar

Small pair of scissors to attach to the pincushion

## Finished size:
4½ x 1in (11.5 x 2.5cm)

## Tools:
Basic sewing kit

Scissors

Sewing machine

Rotary cutting mat, ruler and cutter (optional)

Pen to mark fabric

Iron and ironing mat

Small hole punch

Template plastic or thin card to make
the template

## Instructions:

**1** Make the hexagon template and pierce small holes where marked. These will help you know where to start and stop stitching. Cut six hexagons from the fabric for the outside edge of the pincushion, and two from the fabric for the centres.

**2** Mark dots corresponding to the holes on the hexagons on the wrong side of the fabric.

**3** Take the small pair of scissors that you want attached to the pincushion and, folding the ribbon in half, loop it through the handle. Knot the ends of the ribbon together.

**4** Take one of the centre hexagons and stitch five of the six outer hexagons around it, starting and stopping at the dots. You are not sewing through any of the seam allowances.

**5** Attach the sixth hexagon, inserting the knotted end of the ribbon in the seam so it will be on the inside of the pincushion when it is finished. You will now have a flat flower shape made from one central and six outer hexagons. To make it three dimensional, you now need to stitch the outer hexagons together.

**6** With right sides facing, sew the six outer hexagons together, first along the two sides next to the stitched seam and then along the next two sides up. The pincushion will begin to form a three-dimensional shape, with a hexagonal 'hole' in the middle formed by the remaining sides of the hexagons.

**7** Stitch the second centre hexagon into this 'hole' along five sides only, one side at a time. The sixth side is left open for stuffing.

**8** Make sure the ribbon to which the scissors are attached is on the inside of the pincushion, and the scissors are on the outside. Turn the pincushion right-side out.

**9** Press the fabric flat and start to stuff the pincushion. When it is firm enough, fold in the raw edges of the opening and stitch them together.

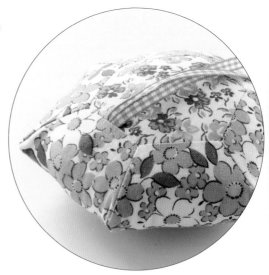

# Tabby Cat Cushion

## Materials:

Jelly roll scraps for cat's body, measuring in total around 2½ x 196in (6.5 x 500cm)

Fabric for cat's tail and head, 11¾ x 11¾in (30 x 30cm) or one fat quarter

2 fabric squares, 2½ x 2½in (6.5 x 6.5cm) for cat's ears

Polyester toy stuffing or similar

Cotton perle embroidery thread no. 8 for cat's features

## Tools:

Basic sewing kit

Scissors

Sewing machine

Rotary cutting mat, ruler and cutter (optional)

Pen to mark fabric

Iron and ironing mat

Embroidery or crewel needle, no. 5

13½in (34cm) diameter dinner plate, or circle cut from template plastic or thin card

## Finished size:

17in (43cm) at widest point

## Instructions:

**1** Stitch the Jelly Roll scraps together to make one long piece. Press all the seams in one direction.

**2** Cut off 14in (35.5cm) lengths. Arrange these into two groups of seven. Stitch the strips in each group together to make two 14 x 14in (35.5 x 35.5cm) squares. Press all the seams in one direction.

**3** On the wrong side of one square draw a 13½in (34cm) diameter circle. You could use a dinner plate, if you do not want to make a template. Place the two squares right sides together and machine stitch around the drawn line of the circle. Leave a gap, either where the head will be or at the base of the circle, to turn through and stuff.

**4** Trim away the excess fabric leaving a ¼in (0.5cm) seam allowance. Turn right-side out and stuff. Stitch the opening closed.

**5** Make the cat's tail. Fold the fabric right sides together and draw around the tail template on the wrong side of the fabric. Stitch along the drawn line leaving a gap at the base of the tail for stuffing and turning through. Cut out the tail adding a scant ¼in (0.5cm) seam allowance. Snip where needed.

**6** Turn the tail through and stuff. Stitch the opening closed.

**7** Using thread that tones with the tail fabric, sew each end down on to the cat's body. There is no need to sew all the way around the tail; it should lie comfortably against the curve of the body.

**8** To make the head, use the template to cut out two pieces of fabric. On the right side of one, trace or draw the cat's features and embroider them with chain stitch and the cotton perle thread.

**9** Fold the squares for the ears in half, wrong sides together, then fold in the corners of each rectangle to make a triangle. Tack to keep them in position, or press.

**10** Place the two head pieces together, right sides facing, and insert the ears either along the top of the head or along the sides, as in the picture. Pin the ears in place. Sew all the way around the head, securing the ears and leaving a 2in (5cm) gap at the chin for stuffing.

**11** Turn right-side out and stuff. Sew the gap closed.

**12** Secure the head to the cat's body. Sew it in place along the curved edge of the body and under the chin about 2in (5cm) from the seam. You can give your cat a very different personality just by changing the position of the head!

# Coin Pouch

## Materials:

8 Jelly Roll scraps, 2½ x 2½in (6.5 x 6.5cm),
  or 8 Moda Mini Charms
Lining fabric, 4½ x 8½in (11.5 x 21.5cm)
4 fabric strips for casing, 2½ x 4½in (6.5 x 11.5cm)
1 snap closure, 3¼in (8cm) wide

## Tools:

Basic sewing kit
Scissors
Sewing machine
Rotary cutting mat, ruler and cutter (optional)
Pen to mark fabric
Iron and ironing mat

## Finished size:

5 x 3½in (13 x 9cm)

## Instructions:

**1** Sew the squares together to make a rectangle two squares wide and four squares long. Press all the seams open.

**2** Make the casing for the snap closure. Take two of the fabric strips and place them right sides together. Sew them together along the short ends. Turn right-side out, fold in half lengthways and press. Sew the remaining two strips together in the same way.

**3** Fold the patchwork rectangle in half across its width, right sides facing, and stitch up each side. Turn right-side out.

**4** Fold the lining fabric in half across its width and stitch up each side. Leave a 1in (2.5cm) gap in the middle of one side for turning through later.

**5** Place the patchwork inside the lining, right sides together. Now insert the casing between the lining and the patchwork, one on each side, aligning the raw edges.

**6** Machine stitch all the way around the top of the pouch, securing the lining and the casings to the patchwork.

**7** Turn right-side out through the gap in the lining. Stitch the gap closed. Press.

**8** Take the snap closure and insert it through the casings at the top. Secure the closure.

# Tips & Techniques

## Note on stitching

• Use a ¼in (0.5cm) seam allowance, unless otherwise stated.

• All the projects are machine sewn for speed and then hand finished where needed, though most of the projects can be hand stitched if you prefer.

• Set your machine stitch length slightly shorter than usual to keep the stitching on small pieces of fabric secure at the seam ends.

## Basic sewing kit

For all of the projects you will need a basic sewing kit consisting of:

sewing needles
pins
a ruler or tape measure
a small pair of scissors
a pair of fabric scissors
sewing thread.

Choose a sewing thread to merge with the fabrics. Grey, tan and cream threads work with most fabric combinations.

You may also find a rotary cutting mat, a rotary cutter and a 2½in (6.5cm) wide rotary cutting ruler useful, though scissors and a ruler or tape measure will work just as well.

## Backstitch

Bring the thread up through the fabric on the stitching line, then take a small stitch backwards through the fabric. Bring the needle up through the fabric a little ahead of the stitch, then take the next stitch, inserting the needle where the first stitch came through.

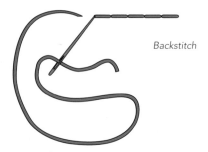

Backstitch

## Chain stitch

Bring the thread through on the stitching line and take the needle back down in almost the same position. Bring the needle through a short stitch ahead, and loop the thread around the needle. Pull the thread through, keeping the working thread under the needle point.

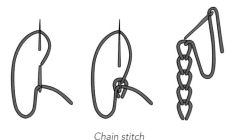

Chain stitch

## Tacking

These are long running stitches used to keep layers of fabric temporarily secure. The tacking stitches will be removed later. Start with a knot and end with a backstitch.

## Appliqué stitch

This stitch will hold down a fabric shape with a folded edge on to a flat piece of fabric. Insert the needle to come up from the back of the work and take it through the folded edge of the fabric shape. Pull the thread through. Take the needle back down through the backing fabric only, as close as possible to where it came up, making a tiny stitch over the edge of the fabric shape.

Use this stitch for sewing openings closed as well as for appliqué. Alternatively, oversewing will hold the two folded edges together.

## Quilting

I have hand quilted all the quilting projects in this book, using a style known as big-stitch quilting. This looks like running stitch, and the top stitches are often longer than those underneath. It quilts up relatively quickly and gives a bold, chunky feel to your work.